AF480914

written by Genesis V. Salmon
illustrated by Nadia Ronquillo

Clay's Adventure To Obedience

Written by Genesis V. Salmon
Illustrated by Nadia Ronquillo

ISBN: 979-8-9921702-0-7 (Paperback)
979-8-9921702-1-4 (Hardcover)
979-8-9921702-2-1 (E-pub)

To my father, Fermín Venegas:
Thank you for holding my hand through the refining fires of life and for bringing light to dark places. Your steadfast love, strength, encouragement, and prayers have sustained me. You have shown me the unconditional love of a father, and I am forever grateful.

The banquet was a success, a night to remember. As everyone began to leave, the Master thanked them for joining him at his feast. Clay patiently waited as everyone said their goodbyes.

"How will I be able to sleep after such an amazing night?"

He stood there, reflecting on how everyone's gowns shined, how everyone laughed, and some even cried tears of joy.

It was a beautiful night. He looked at the empty tables and waited for the Master to return. Just then, the Master bid him good night and mentioned he was heading to bed, reassuring Clay that he was in good hands. "Obey my staff," he said.
"They will get you cleaned up and ready for future events."
Clay thanked the Master for allowing him to be part of such a spectacular event.

The servants came in and
began to clear the table.
Sarah, the housekeeper,
gently lifted Clay and took him
to the kitchen for his bath.

Clay was excited to
experience his first bath.

Sarah instructing
him to wait patiently
while she gathered the
other dishes.

Clay, however, couldn't resist the temptation of the warm sink water and the shiny, colorful bubbles.

He jumped in, **splash!**
As soon as he did, he realized
he should have waited,
as the water wasn't full enough,
leading him to hit the bottom of
the sink and chip his head.

Seeing his reflection in the sink, he said, "Oh no, I should have waited. What will the Master think? What will the other cups think?" He cried and pondered, "How will the Master ever want to use me at any future events? I already didn't have jewels like the other cups. I was already the smallest goblet in the cupboard!" Clay stared in the sink water, tears streaming down his face.

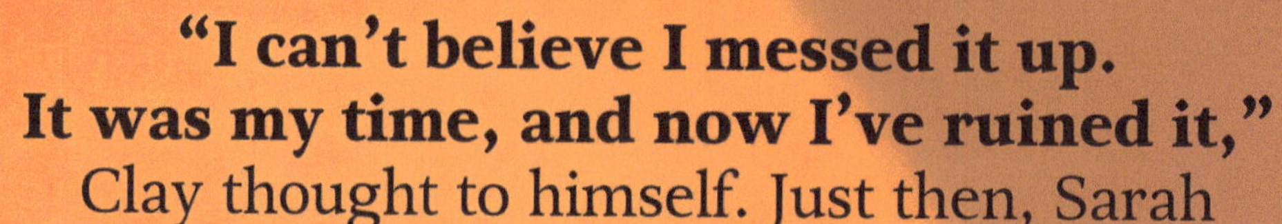

"I can't believe I messed it up. It was my time, and now I've ruined it," Clay thought to himself. Just then, Sarah walked in and began washing the other dishes. Clay hid, hoping no one would notice.

She lifted him and asked,
"Clay, what happened?"
Clay explained that he was overly excited and knew he should have waited for her but couldn't contain his excitement.
"I'm so sorry, Miss Sarah."

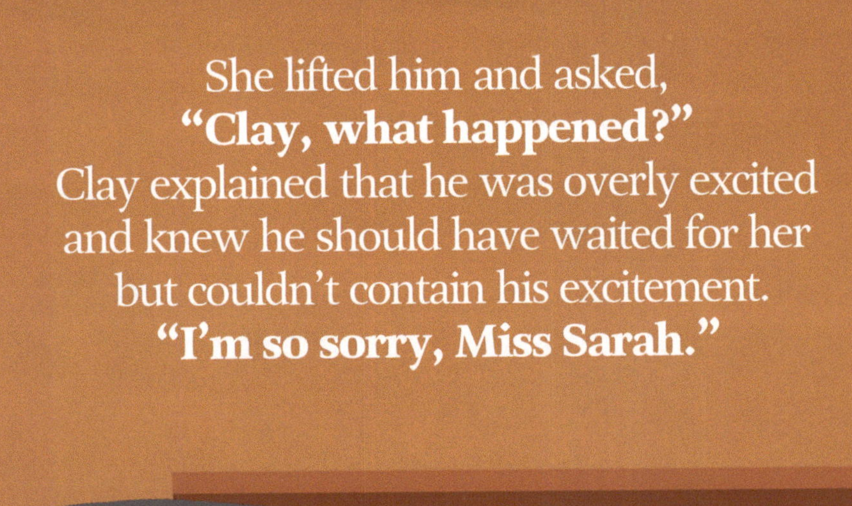

"It's okay, Clay. I will let the Master know in the morning about this."

That night, he couldn't sleep; his mind started to wander and imagine every worst-case scenario. What if he takes me back to the potter's house to live? What if he throws me away? What if he never uses me again, because of my disobedience? As the other cups slept, Clay waited and waited.

Finally, he saw the sunlight shining through the window, and he knew it was morning. He saw the servants preparing the Master's breakfast, and Clay knew he wouldn't be used as it would not be good for the Master to be seen using a chipped cup.
He waited as Sarah reached for a golden goblet. She poured the Master's juice, and Clay's eyes filled with tears.

The Master walked in, happy and rested from a beautiful night with his guests. He sat at the table and reached for his juice, saying, **“Wait, where is Clay?”** Clay watched as Sarah leaned over and whispered in his ear explaining what had happened.

The Master shouted, “Quickly, call the Cupbearer and tell him to take Clay back to the Potter’s house immediately.”
Clay felt devastated. The golden goblets smiled and said, “We told you so, Clay. The Master will always only use his best.”

The Cupbearer reached for Clay, put him in his bag, and jumped on his horse. They traveled back to the small village where Clay was created, and they arrived at the Potter's barn.

The Cupbearer passed Clay back to the Potter.
“Thank you, I have been expecting you,”
said the Potter.

The potter picked up Clay, explaining,
"Clay, when we don't do what we are instructed by the Master, we can put ourselves in danger."
"I understand," said Clay as his lip quivered.

"Are you throwing me away now for my disobedience?"
"Does the Master not want me anymore?"

The potter smiled,
"Oh Clay, of course not. The Master only sent you back so I could fix you. He didn't want to see you hurt so he sent you to me. Then you will return to the palace.

You see, when you are hurt, he doesn't throw you away. He loves you too much to do that! We just have to put you back through the remolding process."

Clay was so excited that he was not being thrown out and would be remolded. Clay smiled with happy tears in his eyes, "Now the cupbearer is waiting outside, so let's get to it. You know the routine:

spin, mold, cut, bake!"

Ta-da, all done!

Said the potter.

“Remember Clay, you’re not broken anymore. You are smarter and stronger now because you have been in the fire twice.”

The cupbearer will take you back to the palace, back to your position as the Master’s chosen vessel .

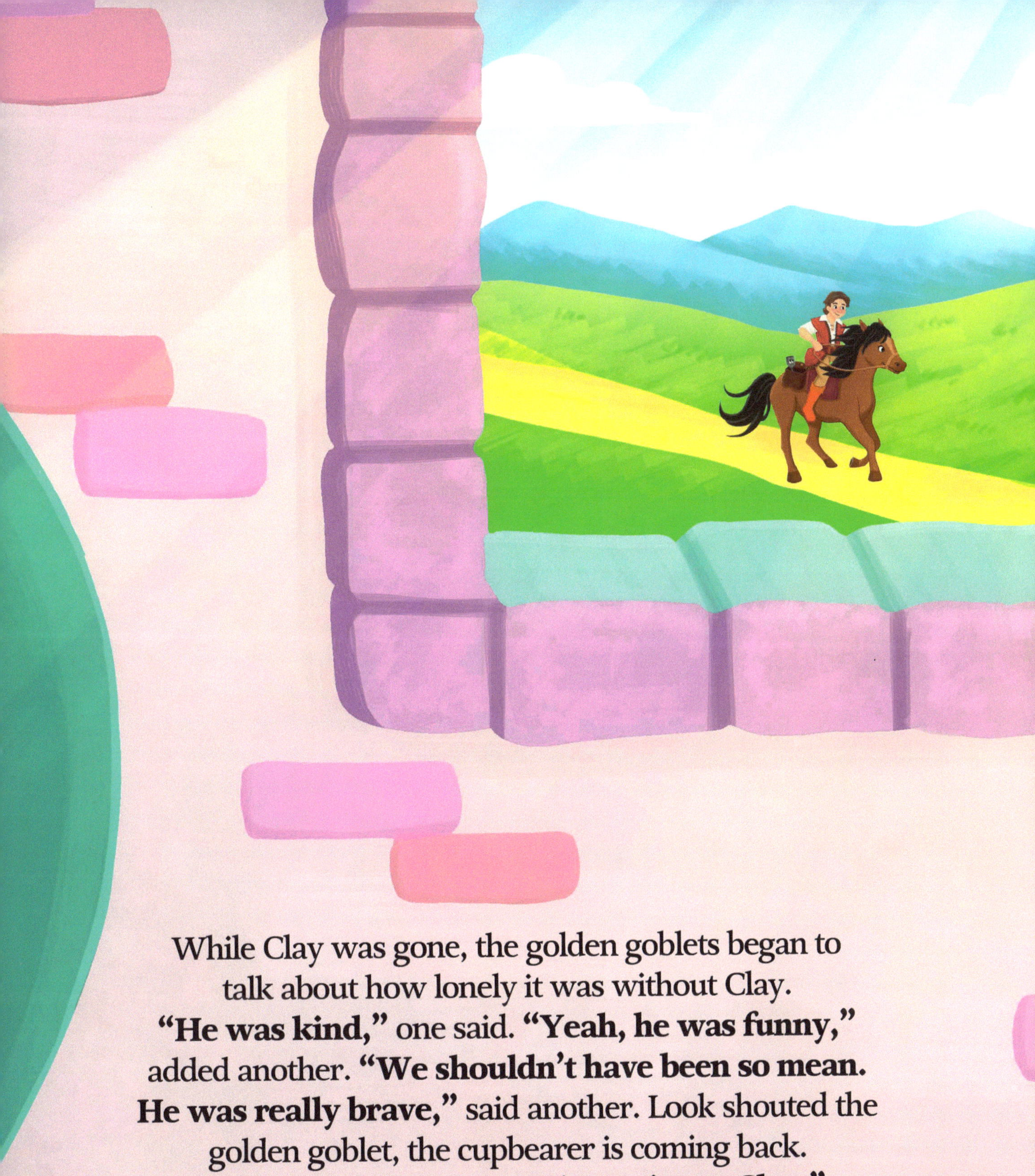

While Clay was gone, the golden goblets began to talk about how lonely it was without Clay. **"He was kind,"** one said. **"Yeah, he was funny,"** added another. **"We shouldn't have been so mean. He was really brave,"** said another. Look shouted the golden goblet, the cupbearer is coming back. **"Oh, I hope the new cup is as nice as Clay."**

The Master stood at the door and welcomed Clay home. The golden goblets shouted,

"It's Clay!"

Everyone sat around as Clay told them what he had learned on his first lesson outside the palace.

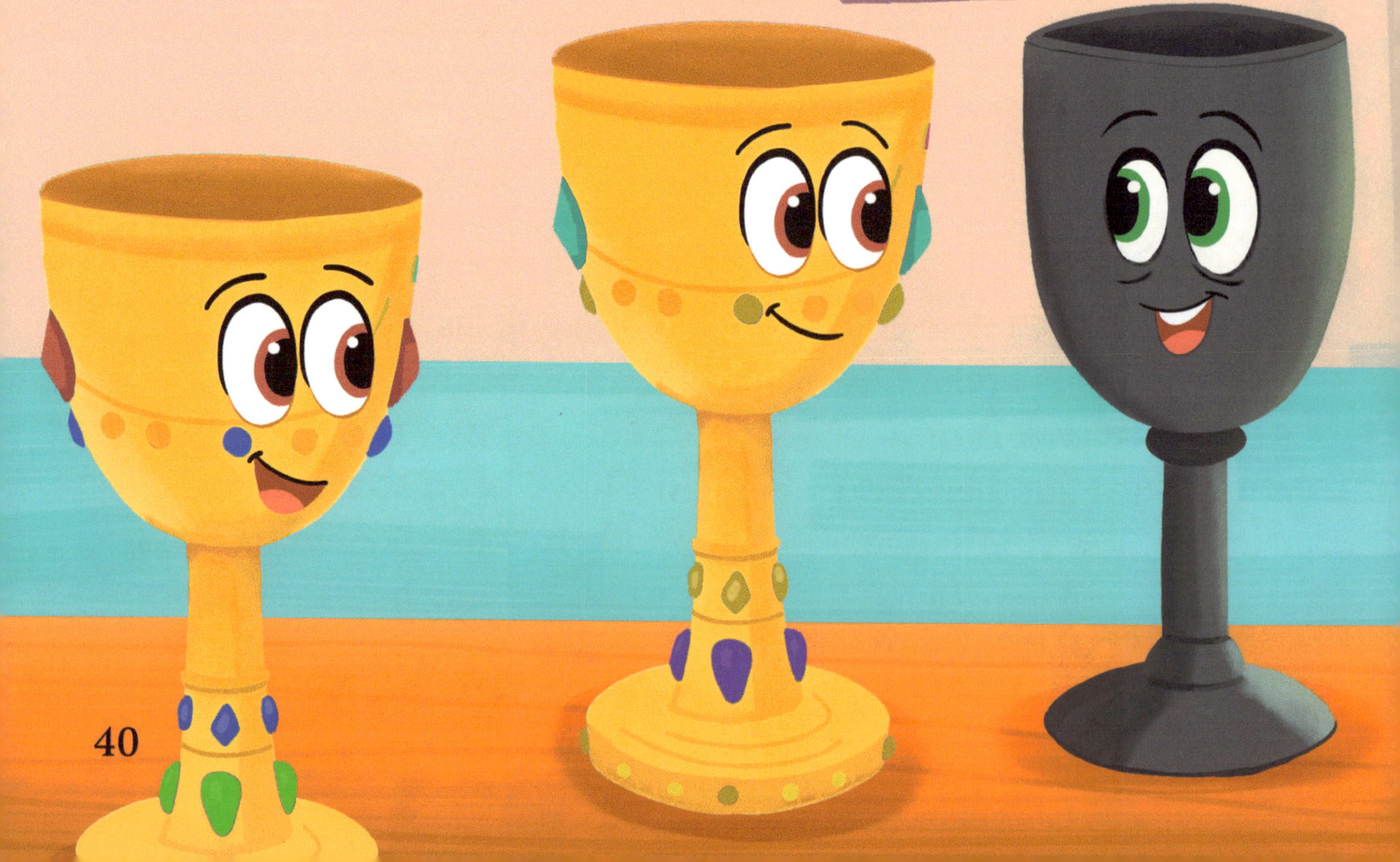

Bible references for Parents

Jeremiah 18 NIV
At the Potter's House

18 This is the word that came to Jeremiah from the Lord: 2 "Go
down to the potter's house, and there I will give you my message."
3 So I went down to the potter's house, and I saw him working at
the wheel. 4 But the pot he was shaping from the clay was marred
in his hands; so the potter formed it into another pot, shaping it as
seemed best to him.
5 Then the word of the Lord came to me. 6 He said, "Can I not do
with you, Israel, as this potter does?" declares the Lord. "Like clay
in the hand of the potter, so are you in my hand, Israel.

2 Timothy 2:20-21 NIV

20 In a large house there are articles not only of gold and silver,
but also of wood and clay; some are for special purposes and some
for common use.21 Those who cleanse themselves from the latter
will be instruments for special purposes, made holy, useful to the
Master and prepared to do any good work.

Zechariah 13:9 NIV

This third I will put into the fire;
I will refine them like silver
and test them like gold.
They will call on my name
and I will answer them;
I will say, ‘They are my people,’
and they will say, ‘The Lord is our God.’”

Isaiah 48:10 – “Behold, I have refined you, but not with silver; I have tested you in the furnace of affliction.”

Proverbs 17:3 - “The refining pot is for silver, and the furnace for gold: but the Lord tests the hearts.”

Psalms 66:10-12 - “For you, God, have tested us; you refined us like silver.”

Author Bio

Genesis V. Salmon is a talented, two-time published author. This new installment marks the continuation of a delightful series celebrating the life of the beloved charater Clay. Genesis a devoted mother of two, with a third child on the way through adoption, Genesis has been happily married to her husband for 18 years. With a successful entrepreneurial spirit, she has established and operated multiple thriving businesses for over 17 years.In addition to her professional endeavors, Genesis actively serves at her local church, teaching Bible studies and accepting invitations to speak at numerous women's conferences. She is also a board member of her family's church in Mexico, named "Genesis the Church", where she has participated in various missions and church activities. Her Christian children brand has partnered with an orphanage in mexico, donating a portion of the proceeds from every item purchased through "I'm Clay." From a young age, Genesis has nurtured her faith and dared to believe that nothing is impossible for God; therefore, she has always been a woman who believes in a big God. Once she became a mother, her passion for children's books flourished alongside her love for Jesus. Writing children's literature has long been a dream of hers, she discovered the joy of bedtime stories with her own children. This experience ignited her passion for Christian literature, inspiring her to create books filled with lighthearted stories and meaningful moments.Guided by the Holy Spirit, she has also launched a blog aimed at inspiring women and helping them find hope through Jesus Christ and His Word. Her mission is to help parents and children create cherished memories through storytime while discovering the power of faith and storytelling. The vision behind her children's book and the , "I'm Clay" brand is to conveys a revelation she received from the Holy Spirit through God word : that we are clay, and He is the potter. Her brand aims to spark imagination and creativity in children while igniting revelation in parents, encouraging both to embrace the joy of storytelling together and the love of God.

One book at a time. To find out more you can visit her website at www.imclay.com or follow her on social media platfoms.

www.ingramcontent.com/pod-product-compliance
Lightning Source LLC
Chambersburg PA
CBHW042051100726
47973CB00014B/214

* 9 7 9 8 9 9 2 1 7 0 2 1 4 *